Time Management

How To Get Things Done in 5 simple steps!

Introduction

I want to thank you and congratulate you for downloading the book, *"Time Management - How To Get More Done in 5 Simple Steps"*.

This book has actionable information that will help you manage your time much better and get more things done. Efficiently managing your time is the key to getting work done on time and effectively. When you complete your tasks promptly, you streamline your personal and professional life.

Indeed, time management is a tool you MUST use if you want to enjoy prosperity in your personal and professional life because when you complete your wok in a timely manner, you have lots of free time at your disposal, time you can devote to your loved ones and other important aspects of your life.

As marvelous as it sounds and as much as we know its importance, effective time management is something most of us struggle to hack. Effective time management is a never-ending battle; one you must fight every day because even the most disciplined time manager often struggles with bouts of unproductivity.

How can you practice the art of true time management and use it to free up your schedule? That is the purpose of this book: to learn how you can manage time effectively to become an effective time manager, get things done, achieve more, and feel more fulfilled.

This book will show you how to make proper use of your time, so you can develop excellent time management skills. When effective time management skills develop into a habit, they will make your life smoother.

Are you ready to unlock a more efficient life? If you are, this book will show you how to achieve efficiency in every area of your life.

Thanks again for downloading this book, I hope you enjoy it!

Table of Contents

Time Management: Is It That Important?

Time management is the process or act of planning your tasks and controlling the time, you spend on different tasks as a way to increase productivity, efficiency, and effectiveness of the tasks.

Because time management is an important aspect of our daily lives, Let us shed some more light on it by discussing its importance.

Understanding Time Management

Irrespective of how much work you complete in a day, somehow, it always feels as if a day is not enough to complete all you had planned for the day. On the other hand, some people seem to accomplish a lot more with the same 24 hours.

How is that possible when both, you and them had the same 24hours a day to work on your tasks?

The answer to this question is 'excellent time management'.

How fast and efficiently you complete your tasks depends on how well you manage your time. High achievers and successful people actualize their goals on time and enjoy amazing productivity because they command and make exceptional use of their time.

If your time management skills are poor, you cannot use your time efficiently; rather, you end up squandering most of your precious time because you do not know what tasks to execute at what time and how to minimize distractions as you work on specific tasks.

Because of this, you do far less than you desired within a specified period.

On the other hand, if your time management skills are good, you smoothly, efficiently, and easily maneuver through the distractions that crop up as you work on your tasks; this allows you to enjoy greater output.

Now that you have some basic understanding of time management, let us find out why developing this skill is important.

Benefits of Time Management

Here are major reasons why effective time management is necessary for anyone aiming to accomplish goals and achieve success.

Greater Productivity: One of the biggest benefits you stand to derive from practicing effective time management is improved productivity.

When you efficiently complete tasks, you save more time; you can then use the saved time to complete other important tasks. When you complete more work in the same time, your output increases.

More Success: When your productivity improves, your chances of success increase.

When you show clients your ability to complete projects efficiently, your performance impresses them; the result is trust in your ability, which leads to more work; your successes help you land more clients, which further enhances your prosperity.

Avoid Frenzy: Time management helps you plan and prioritize.

Planning and prioritizing helps you know the tasks you need to work on at different times. When you have a plan to follow for a day, you smoothly move forward and avoid the frenzy that comes from disorganization. This helps you create a calm and stress-free environment that helps you work much better.

Remember, good time management reduces routine stress.

Better Work Quality: By freeing your schedule and having extra time, you focus on improving your output quality. You discover what you need to do to improve your work, which enhances the quality of your work.

Moreover, time management also requires delegation of authority to the right people as a way to free up your time and direct it to the most important tasks.

When you assign the right tasks to the concerned people, you get better results because when you delegate to a specialist, he or she can handle specific tasks better than someone who lacks expertise in a particular area or field.

Complete Tasks on Time: By practicing effective time management, you manage to get everything done on time.

When you complete tasks and work on time, you eliminate the worry of missed deadlines, which leads to amazing career opportunities.

If you want to enjoy the benefits of managing your time well, you MUST start learning basic time management. Because you now know what time management is, as well as its importance in your personal and professional life, the rest of this book will focus on how to become an effective time manager.

Step 1: Plan and Prioritize Your Tasks, Set Schedules, and Deadlines

You cannot become an effective time manager until you plan what you need to do, prioritize your tasks, create a schedule, and give your work deadlines.

The key to good time management is planning your work and giving tasks slots on your priority index so you can differentiate between urgent and not so urgent tasks. Let us discuss what you need to do to plan and prioritize your work and then set a reasonable schedule for it.

Planning and Prioritizing Your Work

You cannot accomplish anything unless you know what it is you need to accomplish. This is precisely why planning your work is an incredibly important aspect of effective time management.

Planning details urgent tasks, the amount of work and effort that will go into those tasks, the time needed to complete those tasks, and the risks or issues associated with them.

When you learn these factors, you create a schedule that helps you start and complete the tasks smoothly and timely, and come up with effective strategies to tackle any hindrances that may arise as you complete a specific task.

Moreover, planning prioritizes your work. Prioritizing your work means rating and assembling the different tasks in order of importance.

You could go from the least important to the most important one, or the other way round. This helps you become aware of all the tasks that need your utmost attention, which helps you focus on the important ones, which effectively improves your productivity.

Secondly, planning helps you discover all the tasks that are taking up your time without offering any substantial returns (in terms of output) and those that can be done at any other time;

when you do this, you schedule non-important task for other days and focus on the significant tasks.

Planning and prioritizing your work allows you to get the right work done at the right time.

How to Plan your Tasks

Here is what you need to do to plan your work.

Make a Task Inventory: Start by preparing a list of every single task you intend to work on. Do not order them at this point, just write down all the tasks that come into your mind and that you have to finish.

While planning your tasks, it is a good idea to evaluate the various pillars of your life, so that you can easily plan your tasks as they correspond to every field of your life. For instance, some prominent areas of your life could be professional, personal, financial, recreational, mental, social, relational, spiritual, and physical.

You could then list the activities corresponding to each area that you desire to carry out.

Prioritize Tasks: Next, prioritize the list you just prepared. Separate urgent tasks from lesser and least important tasks.

Make another list of urgent and important tasks and rate them in order of importance. This step is quite an important one because it helps you understand and recognize all your important work; therefore, aim to spend at least 20 to 30 minutes on this phase.

In addition to identifying the high priority tasks, break up those tasks into smaller, doable ones.

Quite often, we fail to accomplish an urgent task or goal because it appears intimidating. This happens only because the task seems big and laborious. However, if you break it up into smaller, easy-to-manage tasks, it will not appear daunting anymore.

Schedule Your Tasks By the Day: After prioritizing your tasks, schedule them.

This means you need to set aside a certain time of the day to complete specific tasks. Since you cannot carry all the information related to your tasks in your head, use lists. You can create as many To-do lists as you want, but four kinds of lists are most effective at task scheduling.

Types of Scheduling Lists

1. My Schedule

This list contains a weekly plan of the different tasks you intend to complete in different areas.

This list gives you a clear plan you need to follow each week to get work done on time. This list also goes by the name 'weekly calendar'.

To create this list, take a calendar and begin with a day of the week; you can also use a calendar planner on your computer. Usually, most of us start our week on Sunday or Monday. After determining your week start day, place fixed activities in each block (day) of the week; spread the activities out a little instead of allotting large chunks of time to one task.

After filling in activities on all the days of the week, make sure the allocated time matches the activity requirements you set forth before filling it in.

Play with this schedule until you reach a workable balance. Next, print your list (if you were using a virtual calendar) and paste at different places of your house or workplace so that you can frequently come across it.

Make sure to refer to it repeatedly so you do not lose track of it.

Ensure that you update this list weekly. Making a weekly list is a good tactic because sudden important things can come up and accommodating them in a weekly plan is easier than doing so in a monthly or a yearly plan.

2. The 'Things to Do' List

This list contains the less important tasks you plan to do after completing your high-priority chores.

3. The 'People to Call' list

This list contains names of all the people you intend to call. You can categorize this list depending on why you want to call that person, is it related to your personal or professional life, and the urgency of calling a certain person.

4. The 'Conference Planner' List

This list contains information relative to all the people you interact with on a regular basis. You can jot down all the details related to what you want to discuss with someone and the ideas you plan to convey to them so that you do not forget an important point when the meeting commences.

In addition to making these lists, it is important to schedule proper appointments with yourself for all the high priority tasks. Set reasonable timelines for important tasks and make sure you allot it a time when you know you will be available.

Next, set an alarm for that task in your phone or tablet so that when the time to complete the task comes, you have a reminder. While scheduling your tasks, schedule time for all the interruptions you experience.

There are chances that a client will unexpectedly knock on your office door and you will have no choice but to give him or her your time or a colleague will bother you repeatedly asking for help. Therefore, set aside time for interruptions.

This way, you have time to spare when those unavoidable interruptions come knocking.

Furthermore, when those interruptions occur, because you have anticipated them, they will not adversely affect your schedule.

Setting Deadlines

While scheduling tasks, it is extremely important to set a very realistic deadline. To complete a task on time, you need to know its due date; setting a realistic deadline gives you sufficient time to work on the task.

If a task ends on Saturday, set its deadline to Thursday and start early. This way, you will get ample time to work on it and will have extra time to review the task so you can correct any mistake you made earlier. Moreover, this helps you get spare time to tackle all the interruptions bound to disturb you.

It is important to start your tasks earlier than a few days before their deadline so you do not have to fret about meeting the deadline and you get additional time to understand the task and its requirements.

Once you create a plan for your tasks, get started on completing them. Frequently refer to the schedule and plan you have created and ask yourself whether you are abiding by the schedule; doing this helps you stay true to your plan and follow it.

Moreover, make a point of printing your schedule and pasting it in your workplace and home.

This not only benefits you, it also benefits everyone around you, especially those involved in tasks you have started. By printing out your schedule and placing it at strategic locations, those closest to you find out the important things you are doing and the work they are supposed to do.

It also minimizes interruptions.

Reducing and eliminating interruptions is crucial to practicing good time management. The next section of this book will detail how to go about this very aspect.

Step 2: Reduce Interruptions and Eliminate the Unnecessary

While working on a task, you are bound to come across two major challenges: experiencing interruptions and bothersome unnecessary tasks and issues. Effectively tackling these two i ensures your time does not go to waste, which helps you remain focused on significant tasks and goals.

Let us discuss how to eliminate different interruptions and get rid of trivial things that seek to sidetrack your goal pursuit and accomplishment:

How to Minimize Interruptions

Minimizing different interruptions that crop up as you work on critical tasks is crucial to the success of those tasks. In order not to become distracted and lose focus on what you were doing; you need to keep interruptions at bay.

Realistically, you cannot control everything that has a tendency to interrupt you while you are working since not everything is in your control. However, you can change the manner in which you tackle an interruption.

Here are effective tips that can help you easily manage and minimize disruptions.

Politely Say No to People: If someone comes up to you asking for a favor, you should politely ask them to consult you later and assure the person you will help them out after you complete your work.

This way, that person will not repeatedly bother you. When someone bothers you repeatedly, DO NOT lose your cool because losing your temper will just cost you more time and do you no good.

Minimize Meetings: Usually, meetings do not help you get a lot done; therefore, it is best to minimize them as much as possible. Plan a meeting for extremely urgent and important tasks.

For other lesser important tasks, stay in touch with your colleagues via email and memos.

Work Agendas: Create daily and weekly work agendas for your subordinates and email the agendas to them weekly.

This helps them know what they are supposed to do, and at what time. This effectively minimizes the need to schedule extra meetings, and helps your subordinates understand they should not repeatedly bother you.

Block Your Precious Time: Blocking your time is an effective strategy that helps you avoid getting involved in interruption and distractions.

Set locked-in-stone appointments and meetings with yourself and others for a month and update those appointments every month. This helps you have very less unassigned time; when you know a specific time has a specific appointment or task, (locked to a specific task or appointment) you vehemently stick to the schedule.

Use a Proper Time Log: It is advisable to track your routine activities because it helps you know the amount of time you spend on each activity. Knowing the amount of time you spend on specific activities gives you an accurate view of how you spend your time along with the interruptions you encounter as you tick goals off your lists.

This helps you realize the amount of time you waste on disruptions, which helps you instigate reduction measures.

Batch Similar Chores Together: Identify tasks of a similar nature and batch them together. This helps you minimize wastage of time and improves your efficacy.

Follow these tips and tricks and soon, you will find it easy to tackle different interruptions that interrupt you.

How to Get Rid of Unnecessary Tasks and Details

Getting rid of unnecessary and trivial tasks, things, and details that get in the way of your work is imperative because unimportant things hold you back and result in time wastage.

Hence, you must focus on eliminating redundant and pointless things so you can concentrate on the significant.

Here are some tips to help you accomplish this goal.

Organize Your Environment: Firstly, declutter and organize your work place.

Clutter is one of the biggest factors that hampers optimal performance and efficiency, which is why you MUST immediately get rid of it so you do not become preoccupied with the unimportant things. Start by cleaning your work environment and organizing all your documents and files. Throw away all the old redundant files you will not be using again.

The same goes for your home; it should be clean, tidy, and devoid of clutter so you can focus on the important things and not on all the clutter around you.

Know What Is Important: In addition to de-cluttering your workplace and home, you must also de-clutter your mind.

Detail important tasks and segregate them from those that appear important but are neither important nor urgent. Doing this helps you get rid of all the trivial tasks bothering you for no reason or benefit.

Focus on the Bigger Picture: Quite often, we fall prey to distractions when we lose focus of the bigger picture. This happens when you start fussing about the trivial details and allow them to disturb you.

To ensure this does not happen to you, always have the bigger picture and your end goal in mind. Visualize your goal for ten minutes at least twice daily so you know precisely where to direct your focus.

Open Only A Few Important Tabs: While working on your computer, ensure to open only the necessary tabs because the more tabs you open, the more you become engrossed in unnecessary browsing.

Place Your Clock at a Visible Place: Place your clock at an easily visible spot and enlarge the clock on your computer, and place an always on-top clock gadget on your desktop.

This way, you will keep track of the time you spend on an activity and will keep yourself from doing something unimportant.
Consider these important strategies, since they will help you avoid wasting your time on unnecessary things, and keep you focused on your goal.

As we indicated earlier, you cannot handle everything; after all, you cannot clone yourself or extend your day to 32hrs. Here is where the need to delegate comes in. In the next section, we shall look at authority delegation and multi-tasking. We shall answer a very pressing and pertinent question: is multi-tasking an effective way to manage time?

Step 3: Avoid Multitasking and Delegate Authority

The next thing you need to work on to improve your time management skills is to avoid multitasking and start delegating authority.

Here, we shall discuss why you need to do these things and how you can effectively carry them out.

Multitasking: Why Avoid It, And How to Avoid It

Multitasking does not work for everyone. Even when it works for some, it does not enable them to do a task really well.

Very few of us have the capability to exercise the art of effective multi-tasking. Quite often, when you try multitasking, you do one task much better than the other one.

Moreover, since you have the added pressure of doing several things correctly at the same time, you end up unable to do one thing correctly and end up making a big mess of everything. In fact, scores of studies prove that man is bad at multi-tasking. This is why it is best to avoid multitasking.

Here are a few tips that can help you avoid becoming involved in too many tasks simultaneously.

Understand You Cannot Multitask: Start by telling yourself that multitasking is not your piece of cake. It is perfectly fine if you cannot multitask and you must not worry about it. You can do many tasks really well if you focus on one job at a time.

Focus on The Important: List important tasks and start your day by doing them. If a task or two tempt you to multitask, simply change your environment.

Do not Jump from One Chore to Another: You must fully complete one task and then proceed to the next one. Do not keep jumping from one task to another because doing so will not let you complete even one on time.

Some people are great at multitasking and enjoy doing it. If you belong to this category, understand that multitasking your way through each minute of your day is not necessary, nor does it help you get good results.

Limit your Multitasking to tasks that are not of an urgent nature. For instance, if you have a few mundane tasks to do at home such as vacuum clean your room, dust the table, and do the dishes, you could multitask them.

However, if you have an important report to work on at the office, focus on it alone and nothing else because multitasking when doing something extremely significant is not fruitful.

Delegate Tasks and Authority

No matter how efficient and productive you are, you cannot do everything perfectly and on time. You are human and it is important to realize that humans make mistakes; it is in our DNA.

An important element of time management is releasing some burden and pressure off your shoulders by delegating tasks and authority when need be. When you delegate, you free up your schedule and get additional time to focus on the important, and do what you do best.

Moreover, when you delegate, you discover which people within your workplace are best suited for certain jobs. By allotting suitable work to people with the necessary expertise, you develop various important skills in them, which consequently improve your business efficiency and productivity.

Here is how to delegate authority:

- *Firstly, list the tasks you do best and schedule them.*

- *Secondly, figure out the tasks you feel are taking up too much of your time, or those that do not fall under your skill set.*

- *Make a list of all the people you think are best at doing a certain job and then interview them. Find out if they have what it takes to complete a task and then select the best one of the lot.*

- *Assign that task to the chosen person and provide them with all the guidelines and a deadline to complete it.*

DO NOT repeatedly ask the person about the task; merely ask him or her to give you progress reports of their performance at regular intervals. This way, the person will feel responsible and will execute the task on his or her own.

As you work to become an effective time manager, one important thing you should be aware of is the thief of time: procrastination. In the next bit of our book, we shall look at procrastination and detail how to avoid it.

Step 4: Avoid Procrastination and Stress

Procrastination is time management and efficiency biggest enemy. Quite often, we fail to manage our time well because we tend to procrastinate and delay task completion to an extent where we cannot do anything but cry over spilled milk.

When things get out of control, your life becomes stressful; you panic and in the process, make the situation worse. To ensure you never have to go through a tensile scenario, it is important to learn how to avoid procrastinating and manage your stress.

Let us find out how you can do that.

How to Avoid Procrastination

Avoiding procrastination is incredibly important if you truly want to improve your time management skills as well as your efficiency and productivity. Here are strategies that can help you achieve this goal.

The 10-Minute Hack: When you incessantly delay your tasks, practice the simple 10-minute hack.

This hack is excellent at getting you started with a task and tricking your mind into believing you will only work on the task for a short time period. When you actually involve yourself in a task, you forget about the ten-minute deadline and end up doing a lot more than you expected.

To practice it, just tell yourself you will work on a chore for just ten minutes and then start working on it. Within a few minutes, your mind will forget the deadline and become engrossed in the task.

If you find yourself becoming interested in a task, keep doing it; if not, then just stop it, at least you did it for ten minutes.

Make Positive Changes to Your Work Environment:
Tidy up your work environment and put motivational quotes on
your office wall so you can become inspired to work efficiently.
Cleaning your work environment frees it of all the mess.

When your work environment has fewer distractions,
your inspiration to work automatically multiplies.

Get an Accountable Buddy: It is a good idea to get an
accountability partner- someone to whom you will be
accountable to.

Tell this person your goals and schedule, and ask him or
her to keep a check on you so that you complete tasks promptly.
When you know someone is monitoring your progress, you are
bound to stick to your schedule.

Start practicing these simple, yet very effective tips, and
soon, you will find yourself procrastinating less and
accomplishing more.

How to Manage Stress

Managing stress and anxiety is imperative to staying alert,
energetic, and enthusiastic. The better you are equipped at
handling stress, the more productive you are.

Although there exists many ways to handle stress, here are
useful tips you can use to stay cool and manage things easily.

Know Your Peak Energy Time: Knowing your peak energy
time is important because when you know this time, you can set
important tasks for that time.

Your peak energy time is the time when you are most
energetic and focused. It is a time when you can get many
important things done.

Find out when you are the most enthusiastic to work and
ensure to do your urgent chores in that time. You can use the

rest of the time for relaxing, doing less important chores, and treating yourself to something nice.

This way, you will not feel stressed to work 24/7 and will efficiently get work done.

Set a Work Time: Set a certain period of day dedicated for work and make sure not to work after that.

You must not bring your work back to your home or you will become super-stressed. When you are stressed, you lose focus, which makes it difficult to concentrate on your work let alone efficiently manage your time.

Therefore, always work during your work time and relax after that.

Take Mini Breaks several Times a Day:

To relax your stressed nerves and keep anxiety at bay, take many mini-breaks during your workday. Take a two to five-minute break after working for 20 to 30 minutes. Doing this will reduce the feeling that you are over-burdened.

Keep Everything in Perspective:

A good way to stay calm is to keep things in perspective. You should discern between the urgent and the not so urgent so that you can avoid overwhelming yourself by the sheer number of things you must do. For instance, working on an important project report due in two days is more urgent than planning for a report due in two weeks. When you distinguish super-urgent tasks from postponable tasks, you manage to relax and consequently focus better.

Consider and implement these strategies because they will help you manage procrastination and stress. When you manage these two things, you will become a better time manager and be highly efficient.

Step 5: Efficient Time Management Tips and Tricks

Following the advice and strategies discussed previously will surely help you practice excellent time management. In addition, here are some more effective tips and tricks you can use to manage your time much better:

Use the Pareto Principle

Popularly known as the 80/20 rule, the Pareto Principle is a fantastic rule that helps you enjoy greater productivity while investing less effort. The rule states that you can get 80 percent results by inputting only 20 percent of your effort, time, and energy.

The trick to making this rule work is to know when to work and how to work. You should know your optimal energy time and plan a task beforehand so that when you put in even 20 percent of your effort, you enjoy 80 percent output. Using this strategy, you will free yourself from the burden of working 24/7 and get lots of free time.

Appreciate and Treat Yourself

Rewarding yourself for all your hard work is extremely important if you want to continue working efficiently. Whenever you accomplish a goal, appreciate yourself, and treat yourself to anything that calms you and makes you happy. This will motivate you to stick to this regimen.

Set Clear Intentions and Goals

Be very clear about your intention and goals. You must know your short-term and long-term goals so you can concentrate on what is important and needed right now.

Perform Routine Time Audits

Perform regularly time audits every week to find out how well you spent your time. Doing this helps you identify the mistakes you made and redistribute your efforts and time for better and more efficient time utilization

Conclusion

Becoming a pro at time management is not impossible. All you need to do is become committed to this goal and practice the strategies given in this book. When you do, soon you will never have to worry about managing your time.

Thank you once again for downloading this book!

I hope you have learned about time management and you can now get more things done.

The next step is to start by having a list of important tasks, not so important tasks as well as urgent tasks. You can then allocate the tasks appropriate time then monitor how you do with this. It is important to note that time management is a continuous process and you will always be learning better ways of managing your time.

Finally, if you enjoyed this book, would you be kind enough to leave a review for this book on Amazon?

Click here to leave a review for this book on Amazon!

Thank you and good luck!

www.ingramcontent.com/pod-product-compliance
Lightning Source LLC
Chambersburg PA
CBHW070311190526
45169CB00004B/1582